11/16

P9-DCO-555

- LYNNFIELD PUBLIC LIBRARY -
LYNNFIELD, MA 01940

DESERT
ECOSYSTEMS

by Tammy Gagne

Content Consultant
Travis E. Huxman
Professor, Ecology and Evolutionary Biology
University of California, Irvine

Core Library

An Imprint of Abdo Publishing
abdopublishing.com

LYNNFIELD PUBLIC LIBRARY
LYNNFIELD, MA 01940

abdopublishing.com

Published by Abdo Publishing, a division of ABDO, PO Box 398166,
Minneapolis, Minnesota 55439. Copyright © 2016 by Abdo Consulting
Group, Inc. International copyrights reserved in all countries. No part of
this book may be reproduced in any form without written permission from
the publisher. Core Library™ is a trademark and logo of Abdo Publishing.

Printed in the United States of America, North Mankato, Minnesota
042015
092015

THIS BOOK CONTAINS
RECYCLED MATERIALS

Cover Photo: Anton Foltin/Shutterstock Images
Interior Photos: Anton Foltin/Shutterstock Images, 1, 31; Chris Fourie/
Shutterstock Images, 4; Blake Ford/iStockphoto, 7, 45; Andrey Ivanov/
iStockphoto, 9 (background); Shutterstock Images, 9 (middle), 22;
iStockphoto, 9 (right), 9 (bottom), 9 (left), 10, 17, 25, 33, 36; Liz Leyden/
iStockphoto, 9 (top), 14; Dorling Kindersley/Thinkstock, 13; Colby
Joe/iStockphoto, 19; Micha Klootwijk/iStockphoto, 27; Tim Roberts/
Shutterstock Images, 28; Reed Saxon/AP Images, 39; Steve Geer/
iStockphoto, 43

Editor: Arnold Ringstad
Series Designer: Becky Daum

Library of Congress Control Number: 2015931582

Cataloging-in-Publication Data
Gagne, Tammy.
 Desert ecosystems / Tammy Gagne.
   p. cm. -- (Ecosystems of the world)
Includes bibliographical references and index.
ISBN 978-1-62403-853-2
1. Desert ecology--Juvenile literature.   2. Deserts--Juvenile literature.
I. Title.
577.54--dc23
                                                                    2015931582

CONTENTS

CHAPTER ONE

A HARSH PLACE TO LIVE

S and stretched out for miles in every direction. All afternoon, the sun baked the ground. No plants or animals could be seen. It did not seem as though any living thing could survive in this hot, dry, sandy environment.

Suddenly a tiny desert mouse appeared from beneath the sand. It had been burrowing underground to keep cool. A line of ants, marching

The desert pygmy mouse lives in Africa's Kalahari Desert.

toward a new food source, had woken it up. Usually the mouse ate seeds and other plant parts. But now, the ants made an excellent meal for it.

The mouse had to be alert. It could also become dinner for other desert animals. After sunset, desert snakes emerge from their holes. They slither across the sand or lie in wait to catch a passing mouse. The snakes themselves can become food for larger animals, such as hawks.

At first glance, the desert may look like an impossible place to live. But a surprising number of animals and plants live in the world's deserts. They depend on each other for survival in this harsh environment.

Desert Diversity

The Sonoran Desert is located in the southwestern United States. It is hot and dry, but it is still rich with life. It is home to 100 reptile species, 60 mammal species, and 350 bird species. About 2,000 kinds of plants grow there as well.

Dry Land

The one feature all deserts have in common is that they receive very little

Dry, cracked mud can be found in South America's Atacama Desert.

rainfall. Most get fewer than ten inches (25.4 cm) of rain per year. Desert animals have special traits that let them survive in these dry regions of the world. For example, many can go long periods of time without drinking water.

Deserts are not hot all the time. Daytime is always hot in deserts near the equator, but nights can be chilly. Coastal deserts have warm summers and cool winters. Some deserts have long, cold winters. Deserts can even be found in the frozen Arctic and Antarctic regions of the world. Whether they are hot or cold, deserts remain dry most of the year.

Like desert animals, the plants that live in these regions require very little water. These plants serve as food for a wide variety of desert animals.

Desert Water

Some deserts have huge amounts of water. However, it is locked away from plants and animals as ice. Glaciers and ice sheets cover the desert regions near the North and South Poles. These areas receive very little snowfall. Any moisture that reaches the surface quickly evaporates. This makes these places deserts. Most of their water is frozen and unavailable to plants and animals.

A Desert Food Web

Every life form plays a part in the desert ecosystem. No matter how big or small, each living thing is connected to another living thing. The sun provides energy for plants to grow. The wide variety of plants provides energy for desert animals. Some animals eat other animals. Ants eat dead organisms. This important cycle makes it possible for life to continue, even in this dry, barren environment.

CHAPTER TWO

CLIMATE AND WEATHER

Deserts feature some of the harshest climates on Earth. The small amount of rain they receive usually evaporates quickly. In Africa's Sahara Desert, the air temperature can reach 122 degrees Fahrenheit (50°C) during the day. The ground can become even hotter. Surface temperatures in the Sahara have been recorded at 172 degrees Fahrenheit (78°C). This heat speeds up evaporation, turning

Deserts are often cloudless and receive very little rainfall.

water into vapor that rises into the clouds. Some rain even turns to vapor before it can hit the ground.

Clouds and Moisture

The lack of moisture in deserts gives them very little cloud cover. This allows more of the sun's energy to reach the ground during the day, producing high temperatures. However, it also allows heat to escape at night. This makes deserts very cold. The temperature can drop below freezing during the night.

The Atacama Desert on the coast of Chile gets most of its moisture from fog. Droplets of water condense onto plants. Some water drips down to the ground. The Atacama is much cooler than the

Desert Dust

Desert windstorms can be incredibly powerful. They carry dust across whole continents. Sometimes the wind can even move the dust across oceans. Winds in Africa's Sahara Desert can send dust all the way to the United States. This can cause sunsets in Florida to have a red color. Desert winds also carve the desert's sand into huge dunes.

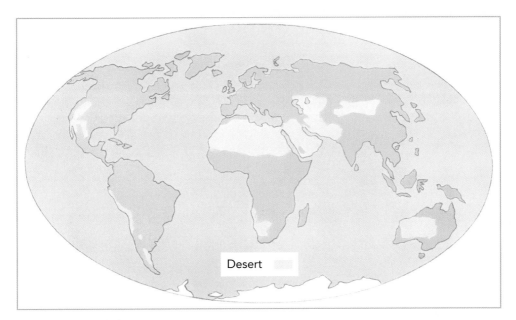

Desert

The World's Deserts

Deserts cover a vast area of Earth. Like each continent, every desert is a bit different. Some, like the Sahara Desert, are dry and hot year-round. Other deserts, like South America's Patagonian Desert, are always cold. The Gobi Desert, located in China and Mongolia, is scorching in the summer and freezing in the winter.

Sahara. The average temperature is just 77 degrees Fahrenheit (25°C). It is still one of the driest deserts in the world, however. Some spots in this desert have gone decades without any rainfall.

CHAPTER THREE

DESERT PLANTS

At first glance, it seems like plants are extremely rare in the desert, but the truth is that many plants grow in this ecosystem. However, they are often spaced far apart. This can help them survive. With this extra room, each plant has a better chance of getting a share of the limited available water from the soil.

Desert plants are often spaced far apart.

Looking Up

Most desert vegetation grows close to the ground. In Arizona's Sonoran Desert, creosote bushes stand just three to ten feet (1–3 m) high. A few Sonoran tree species, however, grow much taller. The desert ironwood can reach 30 feet (10 m) in height. The Joshua tree is known to rise as high as 40 feet (12 m).

Cacti

When people in the United States think of deserts, they often think of cacti. These leafless plants grow in North and South American deserts. They have thick, waxy skins and are mostly covered with spines. These traits protect the plants from both the harsh climate and animals that might eat them. Many cactus species have large, colorful flowers. The flowers produce nectar for bees and other desert insects.

Cacti are part of a group of plants called succulents. These plants have adaptations that make them perfect for the desert ecosystem. They can quickly take in large amounts of water whenever it rains. Their roots absorb this moisture and their stems

Cacti thrive in the deserts of the Americas.

are excellent at storing water. These traits help them live through long dry periods.

Going Deeper

Cacti are just one type of plant found in the desert. Shrubs and small trees also grow in arid environments. Looks can be deceiving when it comes to these plants. They may not grow high above the ground, but their roots reach deep below the soil.

Mesquite trees grow in deserts in the southwestern United States and Mexico. Like cacti, this species of tree has a built-in protection system. Instead of spines, the mesquite is covered with needle-sharp thorns. The roots of a mesquite tree reach deep into the

A Colorful Surprise

Even the spiniest cacti can have a soft side. The large barrel cactus is covered from top to bottom with prickly spines. From April to June, these plants produce beautiful red or yellow flowers. The blooms can appear quickly. A soaking rain at the right time of year can bring out the color in just a matter of days.

Desert trees, including mesquite, grow shorter than trees in wetter parts of the world.

earth. Some can reach water more than 100 feet (30 m) below the surface.

The mesquite tree does its part in the desert ecosystem in a few ways. Like cacti, the tree has flowers that produce nectar for bees. The mesquite tree also provides shade and food for many desert

19

animals. It grows fruit that is eaten by desert animals, such as coyotes. Because the fruit contains water, eating it can help the animals survive when water is scarce. Native Americans, who have lived in the deserts of the Americas for thousands of years, also used the tree's fruit. They ground the dried seeds into a flour used for baking.

Journalist Sarah Shuckburgh wrote about her visit to Joshua Tree National Park in California in 2012:

> Two vast deserts meet in the Joshua Tree National Park—
> the high, rocky Mojave and the lower, sandy Colorado.
> Driving from the north, we found ourselves first in the
> Mojave—habitat of the Joshua tree, a distinctive, spiny
> yucca straight out of Dr. Seuss. The story goes that this
> treelike agave was named by Mormons who thought
> they saw Joshua beckoning them westwards with
> outstretched arms. Late-19th-century cattle ranchers and
> gold prospectors used the wood to make corrals and for
> fuel, but for centuries before, Native Americans used the
> tough leaves to make baskets and sandals, and ate the
> flower buds and seeds. Today, the trees, which can live for
> 100 years, are a vital part of the desert ecosystem, giving
> shelter to birds, mammals, insects, snakes and lizards.

Source: Sarah Shuckburgh. "Desert Song: A Best-Selling Album Was Named After the Weird Yuccas of Joshua." The Telegraph. The Telegraph, August 19, 2012. Web. Accessed March 3, 2015.

What's the Big Idea?

What uses of the Joshua tree does Shuckburgh discuss? How do these uses differ for the people and animals living in the tree's ecosystem?

DESERT ANIMALS

Animals that call the desert home are well adapted to this ecosystem. Some survive in spite of the harsh, scorching sun. These species often sleep or seek shade during the day. Others thrive in the dry heat. Reptiles, for instance, cannot create their own body heat. They rely on the sun to keep them warm.

The desert's reptiles sun themselves on rocks to warm up during the day.

Small but Important

Some of the smallest animals in the desert are also the most vital to the ecosystem. The dung beetle, for example, eats the waste of other species. This helps prevent illnesses from spreading. The large number of species in the desert mean this insect is never without a meal.

Desert Mammals

The camel is one of the desert's most famous animals. This mammal lives in Africa and Asia. It is extremely well adapted to its ecosystem. Camels can go long periods of time without drinking water. At one time, people thought camels stored water in their massive humps. Today, though, scientists know the humps are filled with fat. When food and water are in short supply, camels can draw on this fat for nutrients.

The desert is home to much smaller animals too. Being small is one way to survive in this ecosystem. Small animals require less food and water. One small desert creature is the fennec fox, which lives in the Sahara Desert. This tiny animal looks like a small dog

Fennec foxes can dig holes to create cool spaces for resting.

with huge ears. While the ears may look a bit funny, they serve an important purpose. They allow heat to escape the animal's body quickly.

When temperatures get too warm for the fennec fox, it heads underground for shelter. Groups of fennec foxes work together to build shared burrows. Some burrows are as large as 1,000 square feet (93 sq m). Dew collects in these underground spaces, providing water for the foxes.

The Thorny Devil

The thorny devil lives in the deserts of the Australian Outback. This unique lizard species has many tiny grooves on its body. Each one acts as a passageway that leads rainwater and dew to the animal's mouth. The lizard can enjoy a fresh drink while simply standing still.

Reptiles

Like fennec foxes, sidewinder snakes burrow into the ground when they get too hot. These reptiles live in North America and Africa. Often only their eyes and nostrils poke above the sand. When they must move, the snakes stay cool by limiting their contact with the ground. The way they throw their body while moving allows only two points of the body to touch the sand at any moment. This style of movement lets the snakes travel quickly.

The desert kingsnake of the southwestern United States is both predator and prey. Larger members of this species will often eat smaller members. Few other species kill kingsnakes. The snake can survive the poisonous bites of other snakes. It even eats

The sidewinder snake developed a specialized method of moving quickly to keep it cool on hot sand.

rattlesnakes and copperheads, which both have dangerous venom.

FURTHER EVIDENCE

Chapter Four discusses animals that are part of the desert ecosystem. What is the main idea of this chapter? Check out the website below. Next, find a quote from the site that you find particularly interesting. Does it support the main idea of this chapter?

Rattlesnakes

mycorelibrary.com/desert-ecosystems

CHAPTER FIVE

PEOPLE AND DESERTS

Deserts cover about one-fifth of the planet, and they can be found on every continent. More than 1 billion people live in or near these ecosystems. It may be hard to picture people living in such desolate places. However, it is important to understand that deserts can consist of much more than sand. Some deserts are mountainous regions. Some are rocky areas. Others are made up of salt

Phoenix, Arizona, is one of many cities located in the world's deserts.

Here and There

Many traditional desert cultures were nomadic. They traveled from one region to another instead of settling in a permanent home. In order to survive, they moved to places where they could find food and water. Many desert animals live this way today for the same reason.

flats. Major cities, such as Phoenix, Arizona, are in deserts.

Living in a desert presents many of the same issues to people that it does to animals. Staying cool and finding water are the two biggest summer challenges in hot deserts. Thanks to modern technology, people can rely on air conditioning and plumbing to keep them comfortable and hydrated when indoors. Outdoors, though, the heat and dryness can cause problems.

Every Last Drop

Living off the land in a desert region can be a huge challenge. Desert plants may grow easily in this dry environment. But most fruits and vegetables cannot grow without adding extra water. People bring large

Crops can be grown in the desert, but transporting water there can be expensive and harmful to the environment.

amounts of water to places like Phoenix to grow crops. Residents of deserts can use hoses to water their home gardens, but this can take water needed for drinking and other purposes.

People who live in Chile's Atacama Desert have created a useful invention. They have found a way to make the most of the fog that occurs in their region. Residents have designed special screens that collect water from the air. Called fog catchers, these giant

Drying Out

Humans are causing some of the world's land to become much drier. Too much farming in dry regions, for example, is hurting the soil. Over time many of these areas are turning into deserts. The process is called desertification.

structures can collect hundreds of gallons of water a day. The devices could make it possible for more people to farm in desert regions. People in the United States sometimes collect rainwater from their roofs. This can provide enough water to maintain a home garden.

Protecting the Desert

People can live in the desert without hurting it. But they must be respectful of the ecosystem. In the past, the government used remote desert spots for testing nuclear bombs. More recently, people have suggested burying dangerous waste from nuclear power plants in the desert. Many people are opposed to this idea.

Carelessly using off-road vehicles may harm desert plants and animals.

They worry the waste could leak and poison the plants, animals, and people who live in the desert.

People can hurt the desert just by visiting it if they are not careful. Off-road vehicles, for example, can damage the homes of many animals. Desert tortoises are just one example of species whose numbers have declined in recent decades. In the 1950s, an average of 200 desert tortoises could be found in one square mile (1.6 sq km) of California deserts. Today that number has dropped to 60 in some places.

Professor Christopher Norment explained in an interview why the issue of water conservation is so important in the American Southwest:

Clark County, Nevada—home of Las Vegas—and Maricopa County in Arizona have both experienced exponential population growth over the past few decades. This growth is unsustainable and places increasing pressure on the region's resources, particularly water—and the growing demand for water will in turn affect aquatic ecosystems and the organisms that depend upon them. The increasing need for water will only be exacerbated by climate change and its associated droughts. Decreased flows from the Colorado River and low levels in Lake Mead also pose a problem. California, Arizona, and Nevada all need the same limited waters, and there will be conflict over this resource.

Source: Carson Rogers. "Interview: Christopher Norment on the Beauty of the Desert Ecosystem." UNC Press Blog. *The University of North Carolina Press, October 8, 2014. Web. Accessed March 3, 2015.*

Consider Your Audience

Adapt this passage for a different audience, such as your friends or a younger sibling. How would you explain the issue of water conservation for this new audience? How does your blog post differ from the original text?

CHAPTER SIX

THE FUTURE OF DESERTS

One of the biggest threats to the world's deserts is climate change. This gradual increase in Earth's temperatures is caused by gases in the atmosphere that trap the sun's heat. These gases are released by human activity. A major impact of climate change is loss of wildlife. As temperatures rise, water evaporates even faster. In regions where water is scarce to begin with, a small change in temperature

Climate change can make conditions too hot for even the toughest desert plants.

makes a huge difference. Plants and animals that need a small amount of water may not get enough. Some might get none at all. Without water, life is placed at great risk.

As the air gets hotter and drier, fires become more likely. Climate change brings new plants to the deserts. Grasses replace native species, creating more fuel for fires.

Too Much Salt

Certain crops, such as sugar cane, grow well in the desert. But bringing water to arid desert regions can cause problems for these crops. River water and ground

Fires

Wildfires pose a strong threat to the desert ecosystem. Even after the land recovers from a fire, it is not the same as it was before the event. Fire devastates the native shrubs and cacti of the desert. These species are not used to large fires. Many of the plants cannot grow back following a fire. Instead, other plants may take over the landscape. With so many people living in or near the world's deserts, these fires can also pose a threat to human populations. Dry conditions in California in the early 2000s resulted in some of the largest wildfires in the state's history.

Hot, dry conditions can lead to enormous desert wildfires.

Easy Does It

People who visit the desert can help protect this ecosystem by taking a few simple precautions. First, stay on marked trails. Off-road vehicles are allowed on many of these pathways. The most delicate areas may only allow foot traffic. Other areas may be completely off-limits to hikers and tourists. It is important to respect these rules to protect the desert.

water are used to water crops. Both of these water sources are high in salt. While crops need water, plants cannot grow in soil with too much salt.

Finding ways to appreciate the deserts' natural resources may help ensure they have a healthy future. The fog catchers in Chile represent just one way people have managed to live successfully in the desert. Another example comes from India. A research team in India's Thar Desert discovered that a certain type of fungus may help the salt issue. A part of this fungus works with plant roots to help them grow despite the presence of salt.

Every living thing in a desert affects the other parts of the ecosystem. This includes the people who live there. By working together, people all over the world can help make sure the deserts survive. The more we learn about deserts, the greater the chance they will be here for generations to come.

EXPLORE ONLINE

The focus of Chapter Six is the future of desert ecosystems. The website below discusses how the Sahara Desert is changing in response to global climate change. As you know, each source is different. How is the information on this website presented differently from what you have read in this chapter? What new information did you learn from this website?

Greening the Sahara
mycorelibrary.com/desert-ecosystems

Sahara Desert

Africa's Sahara Desert is perhaps the best-known desert on Earth. It is the largest hot desert in the world. It contains a huge amount of wildlife. It is home to 70 species of mammals, 90 bird species, and 100 reptile species.

Kalahari Desert

The Kalahari Desert is located in the southern part of the African continent. It covers portions of three different countries. It encompasses nearly all of Botswana, a third of Namibia, and part of South Africa. It is home to many animal species.

Gobi Desert

The Gobi Desert is found on the continent of Asia. It includes land in the nations of China and Mongolia. This cold desert contains rocky landscapes. Covering about 808,000 square miles (2.1 million sq km), it is the largest desert in Asia.

The Joshua tree is one of the Mojave Desert's iconic species.

Mojave Desert

The Mojave Desert is found in the southwestern United States. It is home to Death Valley, one of the hottest places on Earth. Despite the heat, it contains more than 200 plant species.

You Are There

This book discusses how farming can threaten desert ecosystems. Imagine you live in or near a desert. Your family makes its living by growing sugar cane. What would you recommend your family do to help preserve the desert ecosystem?

Surprise Me

After reading this book, what facts did you find most surprising? Write a few sentences about each one. Why did you find them surprising?

Why Do I Care?

People and businesses around the world that contribute to climate change are hurting the world's deserts. Why should you care if these ecosystems thrive or struggle to survive? How would their disappearance affect you?

Another View

This book had information about desertification. As you know, every source is different. Ask a librarian or another adult to help you find another source about desertification. Write a short essay comparing and contrasting the new source's point of view with that of this book's author. What is the point of view of each author? How are they similar and why? How are they different and why?

GLOSSARY

arid
extremely dry

burrow
to dig underground

conservation
careful management of
natural resources to protect
them

desolate
lacking signs of life

evaporation
the process of passing into
vapor from a liquid state

fungus
organisms such as molds and
mushrooms that live on dead
or decaying organic matter

hydrate
to provide with water

mammal
a warm-blooded animal that
nourishes its young with milk
and typically has hair on its
skin

nomadic
moving from place to place
without a fixed home

nutrient
a substance or ingredient
that helps an organism grow

predator
an animal that lives by killing
and eating other animals

reptile
a cold-blooded animal that
usually lays eggs

LEARN MORE

Books

Benoit, Peter. *Deserts*. New York: Scholastic, 2011.

Davies, Nicola. *Discover Science: Desert*. London: Kingfisher, 2012.

Sirvaitis, Karen. *Exploring Deserts*. Minneapolis, MN: ABDO, 2014.

Websites

To learn more about Ecosystems of the World, visit **booklinks.abdopublishing.com**. These links are routinely monitored and updated to provide the most current information available.

Visit **mycorelibrary.com** for free additional tools for teachers and students.

INDEX

ABOUT THE AUTHOR

Tammy Gagne has written more than 100 books for both adults and children. She resides in northern New England with her husband and son. One of her favorite pastimes is visiting schools to talk to children about the writing process.

- LYNNFIELD PUBLIC LIBRARY -
LYNNFIELD, MA 01940